AMONG THE CRAGS OF THE EYRIE

POEMS

DANIEL SHAPIRO

DOS MADRES

2024

DOS MADRES PRESS INC.

P.O. Box 294, Loveland, Ohio 45140

www.dosmadres.com   editor@dosmadres.com

Dos Madres is dedicated to the belief that the small press is essential to the vitality of contemporary literature as a carrier of the new voice, as well as the older, sometimes forgotten voices of the past. And in an ever more virtual world, to the creation of fine books pleasing to the eye and hand.

Dos Madres is named in honor of Vera Murphy and Libbie Hughes, the "Dos Madres" whose contributions have made this press possible.

Dos Madres Press, Inc. is an Ohio Not For Profit Corporation and a 501 (c) (3) qualified public charity. Contributions are tax deductible.

Executive Editor: Robert J. Murphy

Illustration & Book Design: Elizabeth H. Murphy
www.illusionstudios.net

Typeset in Adobe Garamond Pro & Copperplate Gothic Light
ISBN 978-1-962847-11-7
Library of Congress Control Number: 2024940406

ACKNOWLEDGMENTS

Some of these poems were first published in the following publications:

BigCityLit
"Tiffany Fountain"
"The Vine I"
"Jaguar"
"Three Bears"
"Limestone Head"
"Handsome Perseus"

Korean Expatriate Literature [American Poets Selection]
(Cross-Cultural Communications)
"This Poem"

Literal: Latin American Voices
"The Ostrich"

"*The Winged Aureole*" and "Statues and Spirits" previously appeared
in *Woman at the Cusp of Twilight* (Dos Madres Press, 2016); and
"*Autumn Landscape*" in *Child with a Swan's Wings* (DMP, 2018).

ADDITIONAL THANKS

*My deepest appreciation to Marcos Alves de Gouvêa, Marta Alves,
Don Berkman, Susannah Greenberg, Elizabeth Hellman, Ana María
Hernández, Linda Herskovic, Patricia MacInnes-Johnson, Elsa Ruiz, and
Barry Wallenstein for their inspiration and insightful comments on these
poems.*

TABLE OF CONTENTS

I. AMONG THE CRAGS OF THE EYRIE

II. BEFORE THE LIGHTNING CAN SURPRISE US AGAIN

III. A Dreaming Head
Almost Lost in the Clouds

IV. American and Other Wings

I.
AMONG THE CRAGS
OF THE EYRIE

THE JEWELED HEAD

for Irving Shapiro

I imagine myself at a table
beneath a tall window where light streams in,
refracting rainbows like in a Vermeer painting.
Before me a great open book
with crisp blank pages where my fountain pen
scratches, the nib disappearing from time to time:
Opaque ink. My right hand loiters,
my left hand writes, fills pages with arabesques and scrawls.
That pleasure seeps through my fingers
as light grows weaker but richer in hue.
I feel myself sinking toward my center, suspended
between thought and act, a deep, seething marsh
in the twilight hush where I carry
my head like a jewel through the gloom.

AMONG THE CRAGS OF THE EYRIE

You, lion-breasted bird,
will find your form
through cry or action.

Take it glittering to the sky,
or bunched in your talon-fist,
drive it home.

I'll watch you glide
from your suspended cave of ice,
guide your tongue
to prophetic sound.

I sit and smoke,
look for shreds of inspiration.
Outside, squat gray buildings
and a dirty mica cliff.

Among the crags of the eyrie
your sun-tipped wings will razor air,
tuck to swoop cleanly down.

After the Storm

Out the window,
a fine point of ice drips
to pools.

And in the distance,
pairs of swans
in white adagio—

watch them scatter through
the nickel-plated sky.

Evening's coming on.
Pink-eyed rabbits, foxes
snuggled under drifts.

Just listen to that wind
through icicle chimes
(a clock strikes ten).

The howling doesn't
stop, reaching fever-pitch
at midnight, blind.

In the morning,
it all starts again:

trees catching snow
in their antlers
velvet to the touch.

A blood-red cardinal
whistling in the pines—
that menthol scent.

Beyond the window
a collie plows
breast-deep through snow

toward a figure with open arms.

LEGACY

I almost never remember my dreams
but in the morning, trees
wave their curly tops at me
and the sky is a whimsical blue
inviting me to dive in.
There are openings and doors everywhere
if I could only see them,
if my feet could be surprised
along another path more marvelous or true.
I enter a copse of dripping leaves,
my image floating in a pool,
a spray of iridescent colors in the sky.
Every direction reigns here
but up and down are most holy.
A terracotta ladder spiraling
from the heavens, deeper and deeper
into the earth, now my mouth full of earth
seeks worms and moles.
The world was invisible, now it's teeming.
Over the land roams my legacy of wind.

THE WINGED AUREOLE

after Bessie Pease Gutmann

In that print,
a girl dances in a garden at dawn,
doves floating around her
in a rosy halo. I'm drawn
to the light tread of her feet
over cobblestones, her filmy nightgown
rising and falling, the snow of wings.

That girl could be my mother
seeking pixies behind the house,
calling her name down a well,
Shulamith—I reach out my hand,
she pulls me in. Grass rustling, frisky
crickets tickle my feet.

She turns perfect pirouettes,
leads me back to a shadowed
doorway behind the cobblestones
cool as limestone, far from boredom,
where hours never pass
punctuated by shrill rings.

My spiraling thoughts steep with hydrangeas,
magenta-blue in the honeysuckle
twilight. Along the sill
sparrows alight and when it darkens,
glimmering wings,
a host of pixies circles my room.

THE MIMOSA TREE

The mimosa trembled like a Chinese lantern whenever a
    plane passed by.

My father planted it in the backyard, by the kitchen,
so we could watch it over homework or during meals.
My mother laughed her girlish laugh,
glancing at the sapling, naked in winter, "such a skinny thing."

By spring, tender swags, clustering leaves topped with pink blooms
fanned the trunk, a self-enclosed canopy, so my father
clipped the lowest branches to make it arch over the roof,
make it reach for the sky.

Those ladders grew thicker and taller every year.

Each June, a bluejay hopped bough to bough, raucous and cawing.
School out, I sat by the window, mesmerized for long spells.
The tree was a parasol, a tropical bird with brilliant plumage,
a peacock dragging its train, a rooted creature longing to roam.

But when my brother started mowing the lawn,
it shattered my dreaming: the hellish engine made a long whining roar,
chopping and choking as its blades caught twigs and stones.

One Sunday an enormous rock hurtled through the glass.

My parents banished me from my spot. The jay
appeared in the highest branches, bursting into caws
as it sprang into the blue August sky.

Indian summer on the patio, my mother stretched out on a chaise, hands on belly, waiting for the first leaves to fall. My father, standing by the grill in shorts and chef's hat, waved a can over glowing coals.

The barbeque flared its dragon-flame breath, then the air was still.

BURNING

An open hydrant spouts the street in summer,
fires trigger sirens, engines, that day in my mind:

lighting matches by the blind brick wall,
I tossed them toward the poplar hedge, watched

the thread of smoke curl from the dark tip,
crushed in a streak of ash along my thumb.

I carried a candle through the front door,
shielded it with my cupped palm, a Sabbath candle

I stole from the pair my mother lit and sang
on Friday nights, when we raised thin-stemmed glasses

half-filled with the syrup she called wine.
I kneeled before the altar of my closet.

The lit wick caught shirt to shirt in its own rites,
where fire undulates the dark like water,

hangers clinked and branded the white cloth
trying to flee, and my brother dragged me

out of my revery in the smoke-choked house.
Behind us gray clouds spilling
from the roof.

~ ~ ~

To begin from the flat, black ashes
of my house,

scuffing my way through
muddy ash ground
into carpet

                            smoked glass
                            with hairline cracks

the burnt fleece
of the armchair's stuffing

                            steering a path back
                            through the smell

of flared briquettes
and soaked cloth

                            to the den
                            where my parents
                            wait,

        to the fork my mother
            hurled at me,

it turns
into a cloud,

                            a ball of smoke
                            volleying past.

Then her question:
Why?

                    I don't remember if I answered
                         or lied

(a horsefly landed
on my sandal   and lit across the room)

I remember her
pale green slacks, crossing
one leg over the other,

                     my father shook my arm hard
                     behind the sunflowers, *Look*:

hairy stalks dropped
toothed seeds

                     into the sandbox
                     where twisted metal,
                     doorknobs and plastic
                     fused like jack-cheese
                     into bull's-eyed glass.

The oxidized bars
of the belled canary cage

                     with its small
                     black coal inside.

He steered us out the burnt-out shell
and our gray Dodge
carried us away

to buff motels
and a rented home
where masonite flapped
the pocked walls,
fluorescent lights
exposed my face
on shadowless
Sunday afternoons.

I wanted to race
across the street
where a neighbor's collie
circled the porch,
the walnut trees
budding
with green fruit.

~ ~ ~

Her unanswered question
rings in my ears.
I still don't know *why.*

Was I rebelling against his explosions
over my foolish tantrums?

When he'd pull his belt off, raising his voice,
I'll strap you one, making me
stand in the hall till his anger cooled.

(He also soothed me after nightmares
other nights, watched over my bed
till I drifted back to sleep.)

There were unquenched shadows
inside me,
dry as tinder about to ignite.

My father's rages, even his love, my mother
floating in the background,
couldn't steel me against myself.

The truth is I didn't know who I was,
turned it all on our imperfect home:

the knee-high dandelions,
the scrawny dogwood in the yard,
peeling oilcloth, pictures askew—

everything slapdash, tentative,

the way *I* felt inside.
My gray mundane world just wouldn't do,
so I'd burn it down.

Was that all true, or fair, or real,
or were my hands just tempted
by fire and I lost control?

~ ~ ~

I destroyed my family's house
and left the dogwood in the yard
surrounded by dandelions,
puffed white ghosts on milky stems
dispersing brazenly in a winged dream.

I defied my father's voice,
a bright seed blasting through me,
childish grievance stirred to greed
I thought I made them see
holding a candle in my hand.

Years later he told me *no*,
it didn't matter, no blame
or forgiveness, the business was over.
The thin white hair on his bald crown
wafted into the afternoon.

My mother calls me from the porch
holding a chilled drink in her hand.
A wheel of lime coasts its frosted edge.
Lifting a straw, she puffs the wrapper
into the teal-blue, August day,

into descending tiers
of yews and rhododendrons.
A sprinkler *chickers* over the lawn,
tossing its long arm of water
back and forth in a staggered rhythm.

II.
BEFORE THE LIGHTNING
CAN SURPRISE US AGAIN

THIS POEM

This poem will not protect you
or fill a room with laughing children,
won't build you a torso and limbs
to cradle you through the night.
This poem won't make oleanders bloom,
sprinkle the air with jasmine perfume,
won't spell out a name on the wind,
burnished skin tipped with gossamer wings.
But a finger tracing these words
might reveal you were here,
what your eyes saw, the music you played
(jolly ballads, serenades, a flight of strings),
what you sketched into fourteen lines,
the grit and odor of your days.

THE MYSTERIOUS THIRD

That other one
is always with me,
sitting on my chest
like a spider or octopus
glomming over everything.
My hand sails out
while that giant sleeps,
dragged back among
the folds of
a smooth gray landscape
whose furred tongue speaks:
"You'll be buried
by my rhythm,
pricked by the needles
of anesthesia
(kaleidoscopes, eight-sided
prisms with no reflections,
falling deep)
until you understand
my vision, until you stare
through my eyes,
bitter as lemons,
and guffaw."

"THE VOICE OF YOUR EYES"*

after a photo of Shulamith & Don

Their eyes
jewels
sapphire facets
that burst into thousands
each seeking its destination
in the heart of laughter
or other eyes.
Eyes bright pools
between curly hair and smiles.
Faces cheek to cheek.
This bond between
nephew and aunt,
surprised in a photo at a family
celebration,
a bond so few really know
(as maybe *I* don't in my nearly 60 years).
Pale blue stars
in a flash of candles, gimlet
hue almost unseen,
like when I glimpsed him
behind the singing
clasp her hand.

*e.e. cummings

THE SPILLED GLASS

A long-stemmed glass filled with apricots.
A bottle of irises in full bloom.
But now the glass of apricots spills,
jarring an apparent harmony.
This still life earned its beauty
when those apricots fell (The violet irises
kept on blooming secret tongues).
A still life printed on a greeting card,
words of apology inside,
words from you to me penned for a phrase
you uttered innocently on a Sunday afternoon.
A phrase that upset our apparent harmony
—conversations and cool drinks on a green lawn—
as if a hand brushed across the table
made a glass fall. The hand was unseen
but you redeemed a careless phrase,
the silence surrounding us,
when you sat down to write those words.

A Boy Named Nahuel

Hugging an Airedale in a garden,
arms draped around the dog's curly coat.

Boy and dog crouching in grass,
clay pots scattered around,
behind them an ivy-covered wall.

I imagine that wall topped
with barbed wire and broken glass.

Beyond the garden, patio, wall,
plastic bottles, garbage in heaps,
a smoldering trash-fire in the street.

It's safe inside this garden.
The treetops beautiful, ruffled by breezes.
Green *cotorras* squawk in the branches:
familiar, unseen.

~

I was supposed to meet this boy,
a distant cousin. I received his photo
with a plethora of others:

Mother and father in their Saturday best,
wavy-haired sister smiling
at her birthday party in a festooned hall.

His black eyes haunt me
as if accusing me of losing our thread,
back and forth messages New York City
to Argentina.

All those e-mails, letters, xeroxed photos
now seem meaningless, orphans,
ghosts.

As if they'd vanished traceless
deep in a continent,
cables cut at the bottom of the sea.

~

In the meantime, he must be grown up.
The house sold, grass paved over,
family scattered, the Airedale long dead.

Would I recognize him
if I passed him on a street in Buenos Aires?
Cafés glittering among throngs of pedestrians,

I brush his arm, and for a moment,
we're face to face.

I see him curly-haired, handsome,
nose jutting out
his bar-mitzvah year

when he first became a man.

Would he light up,
feel a tinge of the familiar,
or just keep walking—

no glimmer in the eye,
no grip of the hand, no tight embrace.
Blood might not know blood after all.

~

If only I could cast a line
into the Río de la Plata, wide as a sea,
pull up a bottle with a scrap of note inside.

In the photo the boy clings to his Airedale,
fingers deep in its black-and-tan fur
as if he'll never let go.

The dog's legs planted
like the sturdiest sycamores
reaching for the sky.

I was supposed to meet this boy.
His black eyes ask me:
Where are you now?

My Father's Bubbles

In the mornings, before school,
with his gold Cross pencil,
he drew faces on the shells of our soft-boiled eggs
before cracking and mixing them with toast.

Or he'd play "bull and matador"
with our mother at holiday parties, poising
fingers at his temples and "charging"
as she skirted around him to applause.

"Let me bubble you up,"
he'd say, before we flew to far-flung cities.
He'd pucker his lips into an "O,"
blowing an invisible bubble around us,
the plane too, to protect each flight
till the wheels touched down.

If he loved you, he'd call you *bubbelah*,
as he did with me and my brothers.
He called our mother his "little girl."
I found a picture of her swinging on a swing,
curly-haired, smiling, from their courtship after the war.
On the back, his signature scrawl:
Sweet as sugar on the tongue.

If he liked you: "sweet as sugar,"
but if you crossed him or he found you
offensive, useless—customer service representatives,
the IRS, the entire Republican Party—
you were "those bastards," even "a moron"
as he slammed down the phone.

Here's the story of the ants he told us,
plastering his forehead with the back of his palm,
two fingers jutted like a peace-sign,
when one of us exaggerated or fibbed:

"They were rolling a ball of bullshit up a hill.
The foreman-ant stood on top.
And when he wanted them to push it left,
he went like *this*" (wiggling one finger like an antenna).
"And when he wanted them to push it right,
he went like *that*" (wiggling the other).
"And when he wanted them to halt. . ."
he'd look straight at us (wiggling both
—a smirk in his eye): "*Stop the bullshit.*"

I recently flew to dreamy Vancouver,
whimsical horseshoe around a bay
ringed by mountains and cumulus clouds.
I imagined his spirit floating in Heaven
before my departure, fighting some bureaucratic angels
draped in robes, with towering wings:

"I demand to see my wife!" he thunders
(she'd arrived three years before).
"And none of your usual B.S.," he warns,
fingers vibrating, celestial antennae,
almost see-through by now.

In the middle of that fight,
he says, "Excuse me fellas, I'll be right back.
I have to bubble up my son,
his plane too, so he has a safe flight."

Hyacinths

The scent of hyacinths floated
over us and you turned to me in the dark.
Beside us invisible crowns displayed
for the Day of Resurrection. Damp beard
against my neck, humid breath in my ear,
whispers. And I understood your fear,
what could disperse us like pollen carried away
on a stiff breeze. I watched flashes
multiplying in the street, comets splash
through desert skies, asked myself why
as I drifted into snores. I knew I'd wake
to your face drained of age, floating on a lake
of possibilities, arrayed at noon
the dangling bells of purple blooms.

Meet Me in the Garden of Stone

A shaft of moonlight ghosts the room where your nude
form tumbles in the quilt's sculpted waves.
Behind your eyes a land of palms and tulip fields
opening to rain: rain hits virgin earth, its fragrance
released, cuckoos singing in the trees snap their wings.
You approach me swimming through waves rolling
into stone and before the moonlight steals my colors,
eats my skin, replaces it with bone, meet me here,
inside the refuge of a kiss, the place I conceived you,
inside this poem.

FRECKLES

for Marcos

Arrayed across your back
like constellations—
I kissed each one,
tasted salt, the sweat of stars,
our future world divined
in warm, fragrant flesh.

I kissed each one
between your snores,
watched the night spread out
before me like a map,
darker and darker until
it explodes into shooting stars—
that Carnival night
you were born
full of masks and tambourines,
rattle of drums,
an anaconda winding
iridescent through the street.

This moment
between two moments:
my gift to you, friend.
But between night and morning,
night and haze,
death could crush
and swallow us whole,
leave our bones on the sand.
It could dissipate
you forever
into scattered sparks.

Yours the blaze charging through
black eyes
when you turn
with the fury of Orion,
infusing me with light.

NINA AT MIDNIGHT

A black cat
left out in the rain,
scratching at the window,
her plaintive meowing
the sudden downpour swallows up.

You can't let her in:
Filomena doesn't like her,
fluffs all up and chases her off
when she slips through the gate.
She's much too dirty
from living in the street.

It almost doesn't matter why.
You tell yourself hopefully
she's somewhere dry
under some neighbor's tin eave.

Every dusk her long legs carry her
across the whitewashed wall.
Scar on her back,
missing incisors
when her mouth yawns open
to accept the smallest scrap.
Her blunt eyes
whet the sharpening dark.

Now the rain stops.
The scratching stops.
The meowing, too.
You call and call for her in the night.

There's only leaves dripping,
the smell of ozone,
a scraped-out sound.

That black cat's inside you
yet nowhere to be found.

Interlude with Birdees
Campo Grande, Brazil

Sparrows fluff in a puddle at my feet—
I call them *birdees* because they're so cute.

~

My favorite,
yellow-breasted
bem-te-vi,*
hovers on the clothesline
above patio tiles.
Billowing sheets
draped over that line
flash in the sun.
He balances back and forth,
precariously tipsy,
claws clinging.
Then he takes off—
Bem-te-vi! Bem-te-vi!—
his morning song
sails into the afternoon.

~

This sabiá,
cousin to the robin,
runs and stops,
runs and stops,
mechanically
pecking the lawn.

She casts an eye toward
Filomena, fluffy gray cat,
who lies curled
on her wicker chair
dreaming kittenish dreams.
The sabiá pecks for
seeds and breadcrumbs
Dona Marta scattered there.
Her eye cast warily
toward the chair,
where Filomena now yawns
—sabretooth fangs—
curls back up, and at least
for the moment,
returns to her dreams.

~

Parakeets
chatter in the mango tree—
from my veranda,
two yards down.
Something stirs them
into commotion,
jostling the leaves,
till they take off
like crazy dive-bombers
wheeling through the sky.
The mango tree empty,
no birds, no sounds,
just stirred by the breeze.

~

Pairs of blue and yellow macaws
cross the courtyard, over my head.
Ironic squawking
as their fringed wings span the sky.

~

"Look, Marcos,
there's an ibis on the roof!"
Needle beak and rounded body
like an elegant vase, flat feet,
silhouette against the setting sun.

~

A rooster crows like a sigh through the night.

~

Now I get it: all these birdees
fluttering above, all around me:
they're *love.*

* "good to see you" in Portuguese

WEDDING PORTRAIT

after a photo by Robert Giard

If I could be
the gold ring on your finger,

I'd sweat and glow
in the cool sun

as you brushed against bougainvillea
cascading down a wall.

If I could be the sweat
that dampens your chest,

I'd trickle and slide
all the way down your torso.

If I could be the belt
that stays your waist.

If I could be the hand
that plays you.

~

This day would be ours
in the shade of oleanders
(bliss among poison leaves).

Hairs stirring
in the wind inside the arbor,

the scent of lemon cologne
bracing at 10 a.m.

I'd place my hand
on your braided arm,

both of us naked
against a grid of bricks.

Our torsos shields
in twin geometry,

our bodies chaste
from forehead to sex,

the casual brushing
of shoulders or thighs

swung in rhythm,
standing knee-high in the grass.

~

If I could place
this gold ring on your finger

beneath a sky
half-cloudy, half-bright,

I'd step through
gelatin silver to reach you,

to make us one
among thunder and leaves

that plaster our backs
as we fall from the sun.

And when you wake from a storm
at round midnight,

I'll lace my fingers
through yours, interlocking them,

before the lightning
can surprise us again.

Dream Helicopters

Now we're drifting
above the tree-line,
the slope of cliff
a sheer drop.
If our paddling fails us
we'll be doomed
to endless falling or
to waking. Smell
the stark mint scent
of lodgepoles soaring
for miles. Exhilaration
at this height, the realization
nothing holds us up.

III.
A DREAMING HEAD
ALMOST LOST IN THE CLOUDS

Postcards from Yesteryear

Pasadena, c. 1909-24

A FUNICULAR

climbs the track
      up
    Echo
  Mountain
then back down.

OLD BALDY

S
now-
capped in
moonlight, tiny
disc on its   frozen
shoulder. Cold. No sound.

MARENGO AVENUE

Shaggy pepper-trees flank the road,
sleepy and shady. Thick trunks
stand in twin, stately rows.
Black buggy with rickety wheels,
spindle-legged nag in the dappled sun.
There's a world beyond these trees,
profusion of leaves, but for now
this horse & buggy hugs the curb.

MODEL T'S

clatter over the bridge
    topped by gas-lamp globes.

They take the curves
    as if tipped on two wheels,

Keystone Cops
    chasing a thief.

They jauntily pass
     rumble down the road

above the *arroyo*
    trestles and riverbed
        dry stones below.

LOCOMOTIVE

Its face
a fierce grill,
steam expelled from
its fluted funnel,
black plume flowing
along its length
beneath a pale sky
dissipates—
The thundering engine
plows the track
rounding the bend,
East L.A. through
Pasadena till it reaches
its terminal, the coast.
An enormous
orange tree crowds
the foreground,
massed dark foliage
dotted with globes,
bright spots
flashing frenzied
stars across sky.
Soon the train will be
echoing silence.
Only the leaves shake.

THE POPPY PICKERS

The young man kneeling
in the foreground
tips his bowler, winks,
twirls his Beau Brummel mustache,
gesturing below,
blossoms spread in a full
bouquet across his lap.

Behind him friends and family
arrayed across the field—
a field carpeted white,
maybe golden in bloom:
Men in stove-pipe hats,
black frock-coats,
women with parasols,
a child in a pinafore
plucking petals off a stem.

They're having fun
on a lazy Sunday afternoon.
Towering over them
the furrowed foothills,
Echo Mountain and Mt. Lowe.
Sketched in the distance,
a faint gray cable-car
climbs the slopes
patched here and there with snow.

The young man
kneeling in the foreground
winks at the camera,
his jaunty mustache, tipped hat,
his flower-filled lap
an invitation,
saucy offerings
to the one behind the tripod
—woman or man—
who's created this scene,

who remains unseen.

THE THIEF WITH HIS EYES

to the memory of Esther Berkman and D. E.

I. JHITOMIR, POLAND, 1900

In that land of cathedrals and poor Jews,
your mother taught you to steal,
stuffing teabags inside your boots,
fresh plums in your pockets sent you running.
You were born to be different
and you knew it, the first boy after ten girls,
they all spoiled you feeding you Kasha,
Russian words in your ears.
It wasn't flesh that you hungered for
or books, your father rolling the parchment
of his scrolls close to the hearth.
You watched carriages turning circles
in the blue square before dawn
and heard another voice calling
beyond the green horns of mountains.
Your feet itched against your boot-soles
and you ran, past the edge of town,
out of Jhitomir, till the sun struck your face
in an open field of barley. There you paused
to hear the Baltic Sea ripple, it was the sound
of your heart roiling your blood
like a plundering ship.

II. WILLIAMSBURG, NEW YORK, 1910

In America, you called them all
stupid, the red-bearded cousin and his daughters
combing their long honey hair. They called you
Yankele Gonoff, the thief with his eyes:
Your gaze traveling over their faces made them
blanch, jump for their wallets.
Every morning, you escaped from that flat,
boarding the streetcar of *davening* Jews;
horses strained against their reins. You watched
a wrecking ball hit the belly of a tenement
and wondered what made you different,
why did windows burn violet while you slept,
the blind flapping like wings, bearing you away
from everything familiar, sod houses, trains,
your pale hands greased with sweat in that crowded room.
You wanted to take them all with you when you left
but your cousin said *no,* shook his sad face
buried in hair, swept his hands across the room.
Every night when you blew out the gas jets,
you remembered their warnings, against explosions,
against stepping out of line. You watched them
asleep in their beds and thought how nothing could save them,
not the god who flared blue against starlight,
or their machines calling them back
before dawn, when you would be gone.

III. TRANSITS, 1920

Dreams, Jacob, dreams.
Were they the stupid ones
or was it you?
Because at least they had structure
inside tenements and machines.
On the train, someone told you
California, and you would stop there,
Pasadena. You didn't care
about the *goyim* or the tinsel,
the loneliness of the *arroyo*
stretching miles as far as Mexico.
In the glass, your face said
me, Jacob Meyer, black goatee.
Was it dreams or a head of glory
you were seeking?

In the beginning it was clear:
When you stepped off that train
and faced the landscape, you sailed your cap
beneath the wheels and pictured
"Meyerville" between the twin blue hillocks,
date-palms, orange groves,
a sea of stucco and red-tile roofs.
You said goodbye to your cap
for new hats, bowlers, schemes,
until the dream became tied up
with something else,
though you couldn't answer what.

Each night
a train whistles in the distance
and you conjure other faces,
other cities, couples dancing
to Gershwin in tuxedos and pearls,
your mother stirring up *flanken*
back in Poland, making a sign on her chest.
You turn east toward the mountain-range
of fog and for a moment can forget
what was lost behind the sunrise,
a peak rising through mist
like your head, the stubborn crown
breaking through.

IV. PASADENA, CALIFORNIA

1928
Partridges strut out your window:
You are a wealthy man now.
Look around this room,
the imported yellow orchids,
your wife jotting a letter in the sun-parlor,
such a pretty, plumed thing.
You line her up with your
daughters in their pinafores
and they beam for the snapshot.

They all laughed at what they called
your "double-brain,"
your plans: to sue your neighbor
because his fence was on your lawn.
That lawsuit started dollars rolling in,
built this white pillared mansion,
piped water from the San Jacinto mountains.

1945
The families you rescued out of Brussels,
sponsoring each with a flourish of your pen.
The Mexican paint-mines you acquired
as if by sleight of hand—
scores of peons you pledged
to sustain throughout their lives.

Does it matter
when you've lived a double life?
Jewels and cottages for your mistresses

while your wife weeps,
daughters sweeping the hall for your feet.

You've grown weary
of all that lying, all those deeds.
Your watch sleeps
on its fat chain half the morning.
The leather armchair
grown comfortable to your shape.

You've grown weary of deeds.
Outside, the wind blows hoarse down the *arroyo*,
a dove exploding from the sagebrush
disappears,
scattering facets of light in your lap,
dust on your tongue.

V. GUADALAJARA, MEXICO, 1955

It isn't over
Your past life comes to haunt you
It isn't over
Men with knives in their breasts
See them floating out of a mineshaft
Spilling blood and your secrets
Down a trail through the Mexican jungle

You didn't kill them
You only used them for your ends
You didn't kill them
You only drained them of their pride
Commanded them with your eyes
Fourteen hours every day
Extracting ore to line your coffers

They were your workers, your servants, your family
Now they flounce your skull
With spikes made of silver and gold

Who will save you
Not your children with their blood
Not your wife, she was frail as a crane
You escaped California
For Guadalajara
When creditors seized your treasures
And *come back*, they wrote,
Come back, but you were gone

Where are the fields of orange poppies
Lining the highway
A row of oaks down a lane in Pasadena
A Russian countess you depended on for luck?

Because Jalisco blooms and breathes
Outside this room
Men with gold epaulets rustling papers
Come to take your lands away

You rise trembling to the mirror
Tug your beard, the world stripped of its cloaks
It isn't over because
The door has nudged a chink—
A voice calling you *señor* and a grin
Letting the last light flood in

VI. PASADENA, 1975

Now dusk falls over Oaklawn Avenue,
over coconut palms trilling with birds,
along the walls of the pillared mansion.
Light sprays along its dusty corridors.
A man lights a pipe in the mirror,
doesn't know what books you lie buried in,
yellow pages grown crisp as old leaves.
This was your house, is his, he doesn't care,
he clicks the door shut on you.
Even in death no one weeps for you, Jacob,
not the families you saved, the workers enslaved,
the daughters you left on Relief,
the ghost of a family scattered years ago,
over the lands you made yours with a glance.

Note: This poem was inspired by a story my grandmother told me about
her cousin Jacob, a.k.a. "The Thief with his Eyes." It imagines his rise from
a *shtetl* in Jhitomir, to Williamsburg, then Pasadena, where he made his
fortune, beginning with a lawsuit arising from a property dispute, followed by
investments in "paint mines" in Mexico. According to the story, he lost it all,
ending his days in Guadalajara, in the state of Jalisco. I suggest that Jacob's
mines and other properties were expropriated by the Mexican government,
which may be pure invention.—D.S.

Mosquito Dreams
for Marta

He's in a bi-plane
Goggles fastened
Snug aviator's cap
Flying merrily over a cornfield
His barnstorming dream
Above a crowd of
Figurines casting shadows
Propellers and wings
Cut through cumulus clouds
He emerges clean
Into a baby-blue sky
The roar of the engine
Hones to a buzz
A singular whining
Some insect around his head
In the open cockpit
He tries to swat it

He'd heard it said
While we sleep
Mosquitoes slip between
The curtains into our
Solitary rooms
With their proboscises
Slake their thirst
By sipping our tears
At the corners of our eyes
He waved it away
As so much fluff
But couldn't wave away

Their pinching bites
A nightly snack
At the whorls of his ear
Imagined their escape
On spindly legs
Iridescent wings
As they fly out the window
Eluding night-jars
Bats in swirling dark

There's a patchwork
Of farms way down below
Checkerboard greens
Rolling hills
A little red barn
With cows and horses
Peaked-roof house
Where some family lives
His life's up here
He banks and circles
Three times
The crowd applauds
As he comes
Round the bend
He sucks in breath
His stomach drops
He pulls on the joystick
The plane now lifts
A double-roll
Plunging down
To loopdity-loop
Somersaulting
Through the sky

The crowd is cheering
Holding up signs
For their barnstorming
Hero, *that's me*
He's never felt so alive
A feeling so
Beautiful he begins
Crying tears stinging

Morning light seeps
Through
Gauze curtains
He stares at the ceiling
His eyes dry
Now drained of tears
That nagging
Whining won't stop

Singing at his ear

THE OSTRICH
feathers and all

1.

Twin drumsticks
tapering down
to two-toed
feet arched tense
on the ground, this creature's
legs like an athlete's thighs
poised to sprint,
or in a different age,
with a little more
meat and confabulation,
Betty Grable's *gams.*
A pair of drumsticks
bearing a bundle
of muscle and feathers,
fluffy wings
tucked all around her,
like a new kind of fowl,
some *churkendoose*—
(chicken, turkey, duck, goose)
But for now, let's keep
traveling up her body:
out of that messy feather-duster
rises her neck,
long and scrawny,
a stubbly liana
climbing lazily to the sun,
high enough
to give you vertigo,

it arrives at
the little fluffed head
perched up there,
way up there,
it looks so tiny
from our perspective,
gazing up from the ground,
a dreaming head
almost lost in the clouds
(how does she manage
that double world
above and below?),
a head both
infantile and prehistoric,
and those enormous
liquid eyes,
batting their lashes
as only birds
(or silent film-stars)
know how to flirt.
Her beak now opening
—an ironic sneer—
but all that comes out
instead of a squawk
is a long, low *hummmmmmm.*

2.

Not fancy-free,
not in her time, not in this photo—
snapped in sepia
at Cawston's Ostrich Farm,
South Pasadena, 1922.
Strapped to a harness
binding her breast, about to pull
two ladies in dresses,
belled white, pretty as you please,
atop a rudimentary cart.
A boy in a straw hat
sandwiched between them
points and points. *Now, Osbert,*
we're about to start,
and the first one raises
a neat birch switch
to flick across the back
of the powerful avian, to make her
flinch and jolt her
into a trot, lead them around
the begonia gardens,
live-oaks and clustered orange-trees
adorning the grounds.
How delightful to be drawn
by a bird instead of a pony,
the second one muses,
adjusting her wrap.
Does she really care
about this creature known for
sprinting across savannahs

in Southern Africa,
outrunning cheetahs and hyenas
racing over the grassy veldt?
Who'd land a kick to a lion's chest
to protect her chicks
scrambling around her.
A soundless fury
builds in her breast.

3.

It happened so quickly
that afternoon, all those years ago,
that plain in Namibia. . . .
like a line of chorus-girls
performing their number,
in feathered garb, long legs
scissoring in unison,
before they were ushered,
as it were, offstage.
And when the great
Mr. Cawston, "grand impresario,"
arrived to inspect them,
oohing and *ahhing*,
twirling his moustache,
gesturing *yes*,
he envisioned them
flocking all around him,
feathers and all,
over the spread of land
awaiting them,
miles and miles of virgin grassland
beneath the snow-capped
San Gabriel mountains.
Quick as a jiffy
they were hustled into wagons,
the ones who fled
were lassoed and herded,
dumped into the hold
like so much cargo,
bolt thrown down

to cut off their lowing,
like cattle for slaughter,
chaotic mess in a steamer
roiled by storms
as it crossed the equator.
Arrived and docked
in Corpus Christi,
then traveled overland across
Texas, Oklahoma, Arizona,
till they reached
"the Golden Land"—
half of them gone,
their frail necks broken,
fallen in scores during the passage,
then tossed overboard
or into the dust,
trailing tears along the road.
Their end
was their beginning
(as the poet said),
these flightless creatures
unfairly known for
sticking their
heads in the sand.

4.

So here she is, in Pasadena,
land of settlers
from Indiana, thrill-seekers
slung with oversized
field-glasses
swinging round their necks.
An exotic amusement
fed whole oranges
right before your eyes:
Come and see the wondrous birds,
the barker shouts,
producing the fruit
in a white-gloved hand.
She gobbles it up
just like she's been taught
as the crowd looks on, the bulge
traveling down her gullet
disappears
(cheers and applause).
An exotic creature to be
ridden or plucked, naked gooseflesh
exposed on her rump,
in order to fashion those ladies'
boas, the ones
they wind around their throats,
fluffy fans behind which
they hide, revealing only
gimlet eyes.
The other prospect is frankly this:
Turned into steak

dashed with Worcestershire sauce
for a "gourmet experience"
in Beverly Hills
or the Upper East Side.
Put the bird before the cart
and don't despair,
I'm telling you this, because
she'll have the last word,
or nearly will.
She swivels her head
from way up there
(point your glasses and see),
looks at the boy
in the straw hat with ribbons
between the two ladies
still making a scene,
looks him straight in the eye
batting her lashes,
that gaze designed for
the silver screen,
emits no longer that resonant
hummmmm but a sudden
squawk like the laughter of a duck
(distant cousin),
grating like chalk or nails
dragged across a blackboard
as if to *teach* him,
teach him something
he'll remember all his days.
The boy's stubby finger
stops mid-air, stiff and pink:
he's lost for words.

TEACHER

for Jan Boss

All those years ago,
in the open
studio at my university—

Faded smock and auburn hair
coiled in a bun, she looked like
a 37-year-old housewife.

Nothing ordinary about *her*,
ringed fingers gleaming as if they were
lights turned low.

She set up a basket
of pomegranates on a chair,

Styrofoam heads,
a few pears,
all draped with an old sheet.

In a childlike voice,
she told us *seek more*
than just a still-life in arranged fruit.

She spoke about
conté and wash
as if they were gold in our hands.

And sent us out into the museums
to see how white chalk
heightens black

in the rounded
haunches of a cross-hatched centaur,
Cupid riding on its back,

how Judith raises her sword
in a swath of sepia
over Holofernes' head.

We studied heads and clasped hands,
the thick impasto
of van Gogh,

biomorphic forms of Moore
and Joan Miró,
brilliant washes in Delacroix's seraglio.

In the studio,
my thoughts ran wild
as I faced blank newsprint on my lap,

felt her presence behind my chair,
pictured a loose strand of her hair,

her glimmering rings
now flashing epiphanies.

She invited our fingers
in that childlike voice, to feel and see,
to break all boundaries—

Then a pomegranate broke from its still-life,
rolled over tiles beneath
penumbras cast by oblong forms.

And in a flash,
I started drawing, my hand my body
finally *free*:

I drew an elephant's trunk
sprouting from a mannequin,
bold in charcoal across the page.

With thanks to Deborah Krentz Johnson, fellow student and friend.

IV.
AMERICAN AND OTHER WINGS*

The shapes a bright container can contain!
—Theodore Roethke

*Most of the poems in this section were inspired by sculptures and decorative works in the American Wing and other galleries at the Metropolitan Museum of Art, New York.

Tiffany Fountain

Look inside the ceramic frame
—arabesques in blues and greens—
the festive scene of Italian cypresses
climbing a hill against rosy clouds,
where a tall stone vase sits on the balustrade
overflowing with peonies
(you can almost smell their delicious
scent as they flutter in the breeze).
Peer into the mosaic pond
punctuated with swans,
twin reflections sailing beneath them
almost unseen, iridescent in the sun.
The only real things you'll find
are at the foot of this scene:
a gurgling fountain clogged with rust
above a wishing pool
glinting with coins like a cup of dreams.
There are flashes far above the hills.

After Louis Comfort Tiffany, *Garden Landscape*, ca. 1905; favrile glass, mosaic.

THE VINE I

Head thrown back
she stands on tippy-toes,
one hand stretched forward,
the other behind her,
lost in a profusion of curls.
The balls of her feet
thrust her upward
up and up like invisible high-heels,
against gravity, toward poetry,
from feet to calves
to the delicate globes
of the derrière.
The small of the back
her center of gravity as the vine
entwines and tangles around her,
head thrown back,
one hand thrust forward,
dangling a cluster of grapes.
She stands on tippy-toes
while all around her
handfuls of grapes lay scattered,
drops of pure joy
strewn on the ground.

After Harriet Whitney Frishmuth, *The Vine*, 1921, revised 1923, cast 1924,
bronze.

VIEW OF OYSTER BAY

As if through the panes
of leaded window, wisteria blooms—
peacock-blue and green—
hangs dripping from a profusion of vines:
entwined against a rosy milk sky,
an expanse of water worthy of
Stevens's "Sunday Morning": Silent, calm.
A finger of land beckons beyond,
headland calling from another place,
another space of stilled time.

AUTUMN LANDSCAPE

A molten waterfall pours over whorled rocks,
milky boulders bound in cloisonné.
Above, a violet pool reflecting peaks,
a sky of lemon and rose to make you weep.
Birch-trunks, sparkling leaves arranged in a bower,
flaming foliage, mountains, sky, all designed for
guests in a foyer promenading to a meal.
What Tiffany named *favrile* and shaped into forms,
iridescent peacock feathers, dogwood blooms,
is nothing but glass chips soldered into place,
light refracted through panes, translucent, cold.
And yet it's something more, something holy or bold,
it's sun and colors melting in a pool,
is something that fires dreams, is glass that flows.

After Louis Comfort Tiffany, *View of Oyster Bay*, 1905, favrile glass; and
Tiffany Studios, *Autumn Landscape*, 1923-24, leaded favrile glass.

The Saltimbanque's Delight

Silvery acrobat in profile,
suspended
against a shimmering blue field—

My mother fashioned her
with impasto and papier-mache,
set her in motion on canvas

till she popped out of
the confines of space.

Her hand now grasps for
a red ball floating through the sky,
a glowing sphere out of reach.

Just like you: once so vivid,
laughing and dancing
through my youth, till you became

pure spirit, elusive, glittering,
beyond sight and touch.

You started as a dancer,
from pliés and pirouettes for Mr. B.
to Martha Graham's "contract and release."

And had your moment—
breaking out of the corps, a single leap
across the City Center stage
("the path not taken," you used to say).

Later, paint became your medium,
your arabesques
swept as brushstrokes,

leaving a trail of iridescence scattered on canvas.

Under the big top,
the acrobat balances on invisible wire,
then bounds upward,
as if from a trampoline, into empty air.

Circus animals beyond the frame
squawk and roar,
the ferris-wheel spins.

Looking up,
the murmuring crowd
holds its breath.

I see you floating
in an ever-present *grand jeté,*
a glowing sun within your reach,
just out of reach.

You're laughing and tumbling

with a saltimbanque's delight
as if you could
burst out of deep blue space.

After Shulamith Shapiro, *Acrobats*, n.d., acrylic, impasto. The poem also draws upon memories of seeing Picasso's images of *saltimbanques* (street acrobats).—D.S.

Jaguar

Crouching,
haunches hugging his bronze rock
body clinging
as his tail provides ballast—

Motion in stasis, stasis in motion,

his bulk slides down
to its gray stone pedestal,

powerful shoulders in constant
rotation like
twin grinding gears,

gears that drive his molten
heart before
he uncoils.

His imposing head,
his little ears
turned toward danger or prey,

his forepaw extends
like an athlete's forearm,

about to flip a fish out of rushing water,
make it flop on shore,
dance in the night

all before gimlet yellow eyes
lying in wait, ready to pounce.

What makes him now turn
from stealth to flight?
(Imagination, what feeds and deceives)

Dense shadow sliding down
into jungle, some lonely canyon,

gone in an instant like
water

     slipping between
               my fingers

before another scene
grows in my mind.

After Anna Hyatt Huntington, *Reaching Jaguar*, 1906-07, cast 1926, bronze.

Three Bears

He looks so cute,
the one in the middle,
standing on hind legs
like a dancing bear,
towering over the she-bears
that flank him. Lifted paws
and little perked ears
more comic than threatening,
their stylized lines
and bronze double-chins
more art deco than real,
arranged there in a happy tableau.
He could reach out
and touch them,
the man writing this scene,
pat their heads
like Labrador puppies
bounding toward him
with sloppy kisses.
But what comes next
when the scene continues
(computer keys clicking,
cameras rolling in his mind),
when the one in the middle
barrels toward him
in those she-bears' defense?
Run fast as
a galloping horse,
toward the nearest alder or pine,
climb and climb before

that he-bear shakes you down,
shakes you loose
like the choicest apple
now falling from the tree.

After Paul Manship, *Group of Bears*, 1932, cast 1963, bronze.

LIMESTONE HEAD

Little spit-curls
frame her features,
like a thirties' chorus-
girl chewing gum—
But besides that
she's on the move,
at least her face is,
the arch of her eyes
and pillowy eye-brows
hold up the nose,
the razor-sharp nose,
it's ever so long,
plummeting downward,
a sheer narrow drop
from eyebrows to chin
like Coney Island's
Parachute Jump
(from the beach, you can
hear the girls scream).
I'm now in free-fall
past skidding cheeks
with hieroglyphics,
slate-blue rouge,
my stomach drops
till I reach the bottom:
her safe prim lips
where the fun now ends
and secrets begin.

After Amedeo Modigliani, *Woman's Head*, 1912, limestone.

EGGS AND SUCH

Poached, scrambled, fried,
over easy—
any way you like 'em.

But not for *all* of us:

My friend L. says,
"I don't crack eggs."

She's a bird lover, feeds pigeons on her sill.
Cardinals fly to her hand
to snag a peanut
during walks in Central Park.

I applaud her,
"do no harm," as the doctors say,
but I can't help pondering
the enigma of an egg:

the fragile albumen
sheathing the yolk,
or its floating embryo,

an enormous eye fixed
on concave walls,
feathered body
growing bigger and bigger

till the fledgling wing
emerges, wet,
out of the pecked-open shell.

Humble chickens
produce our breakfasts
but let's not forget those elegant
brunches at Fogo de Chão,

a clatch of quail eggs
among the endives, slabs of beef,
speckled and bite-size.
I peel and pop one in my mouth.

At the opposite pole,
displayed in a coffee-table book,
an ostrich egg
reminds me of a bowling ball,
marbled ivory difficult to crack.

Once breached
with hammer and nail,
that wondrous orb can yield thirteen omelets.

The thought now occurs to me
my friend L. could enjoy
chocolate eggs
without cracking a single shell.

She could peel off
the paper-thin foil as she looks for
chickadees in the firs,
savor the dark sweet melting on her tongue.

Or she could visit the Metropolitan
to see the Fabergé eggs
fashioned for Czars every Easter:

Enameled green or gold,
vermilion,
crusted with diamonds,
rubies, sapphires shooting off
sparks, mesmerizing as a wizard's ring.

Peer inside this Caucasus egg,
through pearl-bordered doors,
you'll see a string of folding screens
depicting palaces, coaches, ships,
beneath a honey-orange sky,

each scene painted with tiny strokes
as if with boars' bristles.

A whole universe
contained inside a sphere,
or to misquote Hamlet:

"I could be bounded in an *eggshell*
and count myself a king
of infinite space. . . ."

Back to breakfast:
My soft-boiled egg waits
in its sterling cup.

So with all respect to L.,
I'm peckish:
With my miniature knife,
I razor off the top, dip my spoon in,

scoop out the yolk, viscous, dripping,
savor it like sunshine
pooling there as the day pours in.

It's a delicacy worthy of royalty,
even of gods: imagine Helen and Clytemnestra
emerging from twin golden eggs.

After House of Carl Fabergé: *Imperial Napoleonic Egg*, 1912 [gold, guilloché
enamel, rose-cut diamond, platinum, ivory, gouache, velvet, silk]; *Imperial
Caucasus Egg*, 1893 [yellow and quatre-couleur gold, silver, platinum,
guilloché enamel, rose- and table-cut diamond, pearl, crystal, ivory,
watercolor]; *Danish Palaces Egg*, 1890 [Green, rose, and quatre-couleur gold,
guilloché enamel, star sapphire, cabochon emerald, rose-cut diamond nacre,
crystal crimson silk velvet].

STATUES AND SPIRITS

THE THREE SHADES

I wasn't fooled
by the three male figures
reaching down
as if pulled by gravity
toward Hell.
Black and molten, muscles tensed
with the skin of death,
they didn't fool me:
they were the shades
of my grandmother and her sisters
—Esther, Gertrude, and Schiffie—
classical beauties
who thickened over time,
their spirits mischievous as fire,
souls clear as water.
I wasn't fooled
by the surfaces of things.
I knew they'd arrived
to visit their own,
disguised in a roof-garden,
posing as Rodin's famous cast,
come to guide me
on that uncertain afternoon.

After Auguste Rodin, *The Three Shades,* modeled 1881-86, cast 1969, bronze.

THE THREE GRACES

The truth is I was feeling
blue when I came upon
these milky forms
beneath a cupola
in a sun-filled room.
Now, they lean against each other,
the casual play
of arms on shoulders,
trios of legs and hips and v's
in conversation. They have
no heads, the air is dreaming
with eyes of cerulean.
I was feeling blue when I came upon
their forms, light growing
out of speckled marble.
Flanked by amphoras
draped with their togas,
they're pausing to bathe or sing or dance
in this dreaming room.
The blue hue fades
to the clarity of a flame,
and facing a wishing pool
glittering with coins, I imagine
their faces as if one,
flickering on a pond—
Gertrude, Schiffie, and Esther,
aquiline noses, foreheads
clear, the long dark hair
they braid with water—

before I toss in three dimes.
Out of nowhere,
a ghostly voice climbs air.

After *The Three Graces*, Greece, 2nd Century, Roman copy, marble.

HANDSOME PERSEUS

striding forward
in winged sandals,
sword in hand,
from the other hangs Medusa's head,
cape draped over his arm.
He's defeated evil—
the blank stone eyes, the gorgon's
black tongue lolled out—
And regally helmeted,
he's posed as a hero, maker of
myths set in labyrinths and caves.
Nakedly arrayed:
Because what dominates
are his frank, boyish loins,
the dangling stub and its tender sac—
potential for life, desire, sheer creation—
crowned with curls
in a glorious package
encompassing Homer's dream.
My thoughts take flight in my own
winged sandals, freed
of trappings, strapped and ready
for the leap.

After a copy of Antonio Canova, *Perseus with the Head of Medusa*, 1804-06, marble.

ABOUT THE AUTHOR

DANIEL SHAPIRO is the author of three previous poetry collections from Dos Madres Press: *The Red Handkerchief and Other Poems* (2014), *Woman at the Cusp of Twilight* (2016), and *Child with a Swan's Wings* (2018). He is the translator of *Cipango*, by Chilean poet Tomás Harris (Bucknell University Press, 2010), which received a starred review in *Library Journal*; of *Missing Persons, Animals, and Artists*, by Mexican author Roberto Ransom (Swan Isle Press, 2017); and of *Kokoro: A Mexican Woman in Japan*, by scholar Araceli Tinajero (Escribana, 2018). His poems, prose, and translations have been published in various journals and anthologies. He has been awarded translation fellowships from the National Endowment for the Arts and PEN. Shapiro is a Distinguished Lecturer in the Department of Classical and Modern Languages & Literatures at The City College of New York, CUNY, where he serves as Editor of *Review: Literature and Arts of the Americas*.

Author photo: © Elsa Ruiz

Praise of Other Books by Daniel Shapiro

On *Child with a Swan's Wings*

"Welcome to the marvelous world of Daniel Shapiro; a poet to whom nothing in creation is strange, and everything is surprising; who can shape-shift with rare skill and grace, from the deep-state minds of animals, mermen and dream children to the wise guide sent to remind us of the terror and joy of becoming fully human. This is a gorgeous gathering of poems."

LORNA GOODISON

Poet Laureate of Jamaica, author of *Collected Poems*

"Shapiro's poetry has authority, unaffected confidence, and surprising humor. His ego disappears into lively observation and wit informed by imagination. The rich images often delight, from the first poem with its 'triangle swallowing a circle and a square eating its lines,' to the title poem, much later on, 'Child with a Swan's Wings.' While many poems collected here also contain disturbing elements, most impressive and moving is this poetry's human sympathy."

BARRY WALLENSTEIN

author of *Drastic Dislocations: New and Selected Poems*

"The language of *Child with a Swan's Wings* by Daniel Shapiro is downright sumptuous, the poems by turns joyful ('In the Field Between Us'), pensive, erudite, musical ('Rhymes'), sensual ('with these eyes, these ears, / these noses, these tongues, these hands'), visually playful, tender, ironic, devotional ('Ode to Jan Morris'), and altogether remarkable. The title poem is quite simply a virtuoso accomplishment, Shapiro's assured craftsmanship the safety net beneath the bravura. A fully realized companion to his earlier *Woman at the Cusp of Twilight, Child with a Swan's Wings* is a must-be-read-aloud delight."

MAXINE SILVERMAN

author of *Shiva Moon* and *Palimpsest*

On *The Red Handkerchief and Other Poems*

"Themes of memory and desire, apparitions of past loves and lost loves, illness and aging emerge. . . from Daniel Shapiro's bold and moving second collection of poems. . . paying homage to family members, friends, and lovers, whose images continue to inhabit the speaker's emotional and physical landscapes. Shapiro's *The Red Handkerchief* is an effort against erasure and oblivion by creating loving songs of fearlessness and passion, songs of the self in relation to others, songs of the other selves who inform our lives."

HELANE LEVINE-KEATING

American Book Review

"The passionate images and staunch heart of these poems plunge us deep into the life of the body—and the mystery within and beyond it. The poet knows that whatever we encounter—a face in the bathroom mirror, a dead lover's shirt, even a wig, unexpectedly reimagined—can liberate the true self beneath our fears and disguises. Unsparing yet generous, *The Red Handkerchief* leaves me surprised by hope."

JOAN LARKIN

author of *Blue Hanuman*

"The emotional honesty in *The Red Handkerchief and Other Poems* is matched only by its luminous intelligence. Daniel Shapiro writes with courage and grace about transgressions, departures, desire. His full-throated songs against oblivion are also gestures of tenderness and revolt."

MARK ABLEY

author of *Spoken Here: Travels Among Threatened Languages*

On Daniel Shapiro's Translation of *Cipango*, by Tomás Harris

"Daniel Shapiro, with his rich, accomplished translations, has performed an immense service by bringing Harris's writing to the attention of the Anglophone public. . . . Let us hope, for our sakes, that *Cipango* is not the last such project he undertakes."

EDITH GROSSMAN

translator, *Don Quixote*; *The American Poetry Review*

"Shapiro's faithful translations, produced here alongside the Spanish text, do well to mirror Harris's language acrobatics—from Old Spanish to contemporary to vernacular—and choral cadence."

INGRID ROJAS CONTRERAS
Library Journal (starred review)

"Daniel Shapiro has produced a superbly crafted English version of Tomás Harris's *Cipango* in a bilingual en-face format, further evidence that Chile, like Nicaragua, is a republic of poets worthy of international attention."

STEVEN F. WHITE
World Literature Today

"Shapiro's translations are masterful. . . . [He] has found the right balance of fidelity and inventiveness, and he never reaches for a clever solution when a simpler one exists."

ELIZABETH GAMBLE MILLER
Translation Review

On Daniel Shapiro's Translation of *Missing Persons, Animals, and Artists*, by Roberto Ransom

". . . Daniel Shapiro's superb translation from Ransom's original *Desaparecidos, animales y artistas* (1999) . . ."

RYAN LONG
World Literature Today

"Shapiro's translation perfectly captures all the nuances of these strange and seductive stories."

EDMUNDO PAZ SOLDÁN
author of *Norte*

www.ingramcontent.com/pod-product-compliance
Lightning Source LLC
Chambersburg PA
CBHW031218120626
46545CB00003B/902